Facing The
Truth

Facing The Truth

A Biblical look at today's social media

Dr. Tom McMurtry

authorHOUSE®

AuthorHouse™
1663 Liberty Drive
Bloomington, IN 47403
www.authorhouse.com
Phone: 1-800-839-8640

Published by AuthorHouse   07/19/2012

ISBN: 978-1-4772-4016-8 (sc)
ISBN: 978-1-4772-4015-1 (hc)
ISBN: 978-1-4772-4014-4 (e)

Library of Congress Control Number: 2012912247

INTRODUCTION

Dr. Tom McMurtry has been married to his wife Paula for thirty two years. He has raised five children, Tommy II, Kristi, Amy, Kari and Lori. He has five in-law children, Cassandra, Josh, Jon, Aaron and Nick. He also has seven grandchildren, Tommy III, Jason, Abigail, Chloe, Allison, Anna and Joey. Family has always been a real priority in his life and ministry.

He has been preaching the Word of God for thirty seven years. He has been the pastor of the Lighthouse Baptist Church in La Salle-Peru, Illinois for the past twenty four years. He has also been an adjunct professor for the past eight years at Providence Baptist College in Elgin, Illinois.

He was inspired to write this book from all of his dealings with people who have faced real problems from their experiences on the social networks of the computer.

It is our hope that from reading this book people will recognize the dangers of these sites and see how Satan is using them to defeat and destroy the lives of many. Also that people will see the foresight of God Almighty and His many warnings that are given in the Bible that very clearly fit the world we live in today.

Thank you to Tim Thurow for his cartoon artwork.

TABLE OF CONTENTS

FACING THE TRUTH

Dr. Tom McMurtry

There are many good things that technology has brought to us. We now have much more communication with each other than ever before. Yet with this multiplied communication we now have multiplied the sinful problems that communications bring. At the top of this problem list are computer programs like "FACEBOOK" and other social media. In the few years that it has been around it has brought about more "evil communication" than ever before.

1 Corinthians 15:33 Be not deceived: evil communications corrupt good manners.

Matthew 5:37 But let your communication be, Yea, yea; Nay, nay: for whatsoever is more than these cometh of evil.

All throughout the Scripture God warns us about our communications, of our fellowship and our friendships. He tells us that these things will determine our futures; yet, so many Christians pay very little attention to what they are involving themselves in. This book will try and show you Biblically why you should avoid these improper communications.

Ephesians 5:6-12 Let no man deceive you with **vain words:** for because of these things cometh the wrath of God upon the children of disobedience. Be not ye therefore partakers with them. For ye were sometimes darkness, but now are ye light in the Lord: walk as children of light: (For the fruit of the Spirit is in all goodness and righteousness and truth;) Proving what is acceptable unto the Lord. And have no fellowship with the unfruitful works of darkness, but rather reprove them. For **it is a shame** even to speak of those things which are done of them in secret.

Notice God warns us about "vain words." The definition of vain is "Empty, worthless, having no substance, value or importance, proud petty things or of trifling attainment."

Ephesians 4:29 Let no corrupt communication proceed out of your mouth, but that which is good to the use of edifying, that it may minister grace unto the hearers.

People are spending hours each day writing and reading about things that are of no value at all or are telling things about themselves that make them the focal point of the day.

Philippians 2:4-7 Look not every man on his own things, but every man also on the things of others. Let this mind be in you, which was also in Christ Jesus: Who, being in the form of God, thought it not robbery to be equal with God: But made himself of no reputation, and took upon him the form of a servant, and was made in the likeness of men:

This world and this life is not about us, it is about Him, yet the social networking focuses people on themselves.

Look again at what God tells us. [Ephesians 5:7 Be not ye therefore partakers with them . . .]

God tells us that those who are caught up in the world of empty words should not be a part of our lives. Even if you don't write words, reading is just as harmful!

Ephesians 5:11-12 And have no fellowship with the unfruitful works of darkness, but rather reprove them. For it **is a shame** even to speak of those things which are done of them in secret.

Things that should not be talked about are now open news to thousands of people. In Biblical times to spread bad things a person had to go house to house to do this evil.

Now it can be sent around the world with the touch of a few buttons.

1 Timothy 5:13 And withal they learn to be idle, wandering about from house to house; and not only idle, but tattlers also and busybodies, speaking things which they ought not.

If God warned them not to be so idle in their speech, it makes sense that we should not be as idle as to take our valuable time and read and write about things that God calls empty! Families are facing many difficult times today and many homes are losing their children. They are facing financial difficulties yet they find time to waste on a worthless and empty web site.

Look at what God says about a Godly woman.

Proverbs 31:27 She looketh well to the ways of her household, and eateth not the bread of idleness.

Sadly, the only way some children can get to know their parents is to be friends with them on the computer. We have forgotten how to communicate face to face.

Parents spend very little personal time with their children. Hours of precious time is being wasted, memories are not being made, lessons are not being taught. Why? We don't have the time for our children but we do for our computer and our texting.

CHAPTER 1

WHAT GOD HATES MOST

Proverbs 6:16-19 These six things doth the LORD hate: yea, seven are an abomination unto him: A proud look, a lying tongue, and hands that shed innocent blood, An heart that deviseth wicked imaginations, feet that be swift in running to mischief, A false witness that speaketh lies, and he that soweth discord among brethren.

Each point in this list of things that God hates can easily be associated with the computer and communication world. Notice a phrase used in the verses just before these that talk about the things that God hates.

Proverbs 6:12-13 A naughty person, a wicked man, walketh with a froward mouth. He winketh with his eyes, he speaketh with his feet, **he teacheth with his fingers;**

Notice the ways of communication. He uses his mouth, he uses facial expressions, he uses his travel and notice the last one, and he uses his fingers to teach. At the time Proverbs was written, this may have been referring to some kind of hand gestures, but looking at our world today, I see people using their fingers to text on their phones and type on their computers messages that God tells us He hates. It is even more than what we consider as hate. It is what God calls an abomination. The word abomination means "extreme hatred," God is telling us that He hates all these things with an extreme hatred.

A Proud Look: Facebook photos are often all about self. This is their chance to be the model they could never be in the world before. Now everyone can see how beautiful or handsome they are. The world can see my great accomplishments no matter how small it is the world can now see it! Look at me! God hates it!

Psalms 10:4 The wicked, through the pride of his countenance, will not seek after God: God is not in all his thoughts.

Psalms 73:6-8 Therefore pride compasseth them about as a chain; violence covereth them as a garment. Their eyes stand out with fatness: they have more than heart could wish. They are corrupt, and speak wickedly concerning oppression: they speak loftily.

A Lying Tongue: People posting things that are not true or maybe just partially true. It could be they don't realize the lie they are spreading because they believe someone else who is lying yet it is posted, the lie is out and it cannot be brought back again. God hates it!

Proverbs 12:22 Lying lips are abomination to the LORD: but they that deal truly are his delight.

Proverbs 26:28 A lying tongue hateth those that are afflicted by it; and a flattering mouth worketh ruin.

John 8:44 Ye are of your father the devil, and the lusts of your father ye will do. He was a murderer from the beginning, and abode not in the truth, because there is no truth in him. When he speaketh a lie, he speaketh of his own: **for he is a liar, and the father of it.**

Hands That Shed Innocent Blood: This can go along with the lies that are told that hurt the reputation of an innocent person. But you found them guilty on your own so you can share it with others who will now think evil of that person. They may not physically be killed but their name and reputation have been killed by someone who can now share with the world what is in their heart against another. God hates it!

Isaiah 59:3-6 For your hands are defiled with blood, and your fingers with iniquity; your lips have spoken lies, your tongue hath muttered perverseness. None calleth for justice, nor any pleadeth for truth: they trust in vanity, and speak lies; they conceive mischief, and bring forth iniquity. They hatch cockatrice' eggs, and weave the spider's web: he that eateth of their eggs dieth, and that which is crushed breaketh out into a viper. Their webs shall not become garments, neither shall they cover themselves with their works: their works are works of iniquity, and the act of violence is in their hands.

An Heart That Deviseth Wicked Imaginations: How often do we hear of marriages breaking up because old relationships are renewed on the computer. Young people lose their purity from finding someone with the same wicked thoughts in their mind on the computer. Plans are made by young people to go against the rules of their parents because of the imaginations shared on the computer. God hates it!

Zechariah 8:17 And let none of you imagine evil in your hearts against his neighbour; and love no false oath: for all these are things that I hate, saith the LORD.

Micah 2:1 Woe to them that devise iniquity, and work evil upon their beds! when the morning is light, they practise it, because it is in the power of their hand.

Feet That Be Swift In Running To Mischief: Now with the computers and phones we carry with us, plans to do something wrong can be swiftly shared and before they have had time to think it over or get permission from their family they find themselves running into the mischief. God hates it!

Isaiah 59:7 Their feet run to evil, and they make haste to shed innocent blood: their thoughts are thoughts of iniquity; wasting and destruction are in their paths.

A False Witness That Speaketh Lies: The false witness can send out the lie much faster and much sooner and to many more people. They can tell a truth but it may not be the whole truth and it still does the damage of a total lie! God hates it!

Proverbs 19:5 A false witness shall not be unpunished, and he that speaketh lies shall not escape.

Proverbs 25:18 A man that beareth false witness against his neighbour is a maul, and a sword, and a sharp arrow.

Matthew 15:19 For out of the heart proceed evil thoughts, murders, adulteries, fornications, thefts, false witness, blasphemies:

He That Soweth Discord Among The Brethren: This is anything that cause problems or disagreement among the brethren. That is the people of God. One of the main problems with these computer sites is the viruses that are spread. I am not talking about computer viruses but church viruses and family viruses. As a pastor, I have had to deal with many issues that have come up through these computer programs. I can truly see why God in His infinite wisdom made the statement calling it an abomination. How can people take part in things like these that God ranks with homosexuality and witchcraft?

Leviticus 18:22 Thou shalt not lie with mankind, as with womankind: it is abomination.

Leviticus 20:13 If a man also lie with mankind, as he lieth with a woman, both of them have committed an abomination: they shall surely be put to death; their blood shall be upon them.

Deuteronomy 18:10-12 There shall not be found among you any one that maketh his son or his daughter to pass through the fire, or that useth divination, or an observer of times, or an enchanter, or a witch, Or a charmer, or a consulter with familiar spirits, or a wizard, or a necromancer. For all that do these things are an abomination unto the LORD: and because of these abominations the LORD thy God doth drive them out from before thee.

This may be more dangerous because people don't see this evil like the evil of the other abominations that stand out so clearly in their eyes. They cannot see that the gossip and the discord spreading is causing God to become as angry at them as He does at those who commit these other sins. Though people would not get involved with witchcraft or with sexual abominations they are easily led into the abomination that God list as the one He hates the most. Sowing discord among the brethren!

James 3:14-16 But if ye have bitter envying and strife in your hearts, glory not, and lie not against the truth. This wisdom descendeth not from above, but is earthly, sensual, devilish. For where envying and strife is, there is confusion and every evil work.

"This year my family decided to celebrate the New Year together on Facebook. Uncle Larry had an argument with Grandma, Aunt Mary was upset with something that she saw in Judy's profile. My mom was upset because no one clicked "like" for any of the photos she posted. I got so bored that I switched over to Twitter to talk to my friends. It turned out to be a normal family gathering after all!"

TWT

CHAPTER 2

SOCIAL NETWORK ADDICTION

2 Peter 2:22 But it is happened unto them according to the true proverb, The dog is turned to his own vomit again; and the sow that was washed to her wallowing in the mire.

Sadly the social networking world is becoming an addiction to many people. Even when they see the pain and problems that come with it, they are still drawn to it is such a powerful way that they feel they cannot survive without contact with it. Much like the alcoholic or the drug addict who realizes that what they are doing is hurting them and their family, they cannot stop themselves from doing what makes them feel good for a moment even though it is destroying their future. Recently, I counseled a family with a mother who had recently been imprisoned because of her drug addiction. They told me how she could not stop herself from using the drugs. They were actually glad that she was sent to prison. They thought that this might give her a chance to overcome her addictions.

They also told me that her addiction was not only to the drug but to the needle that she used to inject the drug. There were times she would sit and poke herself with the needle. If she didn't have the drug she was at least going to feel the pain of the injection, some how this brought her comfort.

For those who are not addicted to drugs, this makes little sense. Why would someone sit and hurt themselves in order to bring themselves comfort? I do not know the answer to that question, nor do I understand why people would be so involved in social networking that they end up hurting themselves. They see the suffering and pain all around them, but they cannot stop themselves from doing what is likely to destroy them.

Proverbs 23:35 They have stricken me, shalt thou say, and I was not sick; they have beaten me, and I felt it not: when shall I awake? I will seek it yet again.

The definition of the word *addict* in the Webster's 1828 dictionary is: "Devoted by customary practice." There are millions of people who feel they must be on their computer or phone every day. Many cannot go a few hours without seeing the post that is added by their friends or adding something to their own page. Lately in the news I have heard of people who are so caught up in social networking that they spend as many hours online as they do working their jobs. Marriages are breaking up, parents are losing their children. Why? "I have to be online!" "It is more important to have a lot of Facebook friends than it is to build a proper relationship with my mate, my children, or my God!"

It would be wonderful if people were as devoted to God, the Bible, and Church as they are to these.

1 Corinthians 15:33-34 Be not deceived: **evil communications corrupt good manners.** Awake to righteousness, and sin not; for some have not the knowledge of God: I speak this to your shame.

God warns us throughout the scripture of the dangers of bad communications. He tells us that it will corrupt the good that is in us. Words have so much more power than most realize.

Ephesians 5:6-7 Let no man deceive you **with vain words**: for because of these things cometh the wrath of God upon the children of disobedience. Be not ye therefore **partakers with them.**

It is not just the words we say but the words we hear and read.

God tells us that we should not be deceived by "vain words." The word *vain* is defined as: Empty, worthless, having no substance, value or importance.

Most can't seem to find the time to read the Word's of God, but will devotedly read the words of "friends" that have little or no substance. We have to know how their day is going, but we care very little about what the Holy Spirit of God want to give us from the Bible.

People can memorize all the e mail addresses and profile names yet they cannot take time to memorize the scripture. God tells us not to be partakers with them. He is telling us clearly that He doesn't want us to be caught up with those who focus on things that are empty or that are disobedient to His Word. Remember the definition of addiction: "Devoted by customary practice." Is it your custom to be involved in these communication programs every day? Would your friends be shocked not to see your daily post? Can you see yourself not on Facebook? Are you devoted to your computer and your phone?

Remember, God is all knowing and when He gave us the Scripture, He saw that the future would be what it is today. He knew the problems that would come in the world we are living in today. As you read the Bible, you should notice all that God teaches us about our communications. It should cause you to be very careful in what it is you are "addicted to."

Addictions come to lives because there is such a feeling in their mind and body that one is willing to sacrifice everything for that feeling. Paul gives us some good advice about our bodies.

1 Corinthians 9:27 But I keep under my body, and bring it into subjection: lest that by any means, when I have preached to others, I myself should be a castaway.

He tells us that our bodies must be brought into subjection. All of our bodies want to do things that are not good. So we must work on having a stronger spirit. When the great King David decided to stay home from a battle, his eyes saw something he shouldn't have. Then he made a decision to do something that he knew was wrong. He slept with Bathsheba. She got pregnant, so now he made a decision to try and cover his sin by sending for her husband to come home. This cover up didn't work so now he decides to have him killed. He now marries the woman and feels that everything is alright, till a prophet comes and point out what seems to be another man's sin. This angers David so much that he demands the man face judgment. The prophet points out to David that he is the man.

David sees his sin and he prays for God's forgiveness. He now sees where the problem started. He made the bad fleshly decisions because his spirit was not right.

Psalms 51:10 Create in me a clean heart, O God; and renew **a right spirit within me.**

Many people today are now physically addicted to this new social communicative system. It is bringing pleasures to their mind and body that no matter what the consequences may be they cannot stop. Most cannot even bring themselves to stop for a day; many cannot stop for an hour.

I recently heard a news report of people who are texting in their sleep! They are so hooked on communicating that even when their eyes close in sleep their fingers keep pushing the texting buttons.

Perhaps this is one of the reasons Christ tells us to fast and pray. He knows that our bodies will always be at battle with our spirit. If we can keep our bodies from eating we can learn to control other temptations our bodies throw at us.

A good way to tell if you have an addiction to your phone and computer would be to take some time away from it. See if you can go a week without your computer or phone. Sadly most people cannot even go one day without going through withdrawals.

Another sad thing about addiction is that the addict cannot see the addiction themselves. If they are to be helped there has to be someone that will intervene and point out the problem. That is what I hope will happen as social network addicts read this. They will finally see where they are going and will seek the help that they need.

My stomach keeps making this googling sound, and my heart always feels twittery!

You need to stay off of the internet!!!

CHAPTER 3

YOU ARE NOW OR SOON SHALL BE WHAT YOUR FRIENDS ARE

Proverbs 22:24-25 Make **no friendship** with an angry man; and with a furious man thou shalt not go: **Lest thou learn his ways**, and get a snare to thy soul.

James 4:4-5 Ye adulterers and adulteresses, know ye not that the friendship of the world is enmity with God? whosoever therefore will be **a friend of the world is the enemy of God.** Do ye think that the scripture saith in vain, The spirit that dwelleth in us lusteth to envy?

Many years ago I heard a preacher make the statement, "You are now or soon shall be what your friends are." The message he gave that day helped me so much through out my life. I have seen that statement come true hundreds of times in my ministry. If you are with people that are doing wrong, soon you will be doing wrong. God tells us in the Bible that if we are friends with the world we are at enmity with Him. The word *enmity* is defined as: The opposite of friendship, ill will, hatred, unfriendly disposition.

These are very strong words that ought to make us very careful who it is we consider a friend. How can I have a close relationship with someone who has a bad relationship with my God? God says that the spirit in us lusteth to envy. God looks at all we do with these friends who want nothing to do with Him, and it causes Him great pain.

How would you feel if someone you considered a friend was close friends with someone who hated you and wanted to hurt you? You would wonder if that person was really your friend. That is what God is telling us. We should only be friends with those who are His friends!

1 John 2:15-16 Love not the world, neither the things that are in the world. If any man love the world, the love of the Father is not in him. For all that is in the world, the lust of the flesh, and the lust of the eyes, and the pride of life, is not of the Father, but is of the world.

God tells us very plainly that we are not to love the world! If our love and attraction is toward this world, that shows us clearly that our love for God is not what it ought to be. Notice the three phrases God gives us.

First: *"The Lust of the Flesh."* So many people make decisions in life based on how something makes them feel physically. Remember the old statement, "If it feels good, do it." This is where many believers are today. It does not matter what the Word of God says, what matters to them is what they feel. If they like it, it must be OK. As you look at your friendship list, ask yourself the question; "Are my friends, friends of God?" It is not just what you write and talk about, but what are your friends writing and taking about? Remember, you are what your friends are.

Second: *"The Lust of the Eyes."* What is it our eyes desire to see? The things we see end up becoming a desire of our flesh and what we see and desire we soon begin to do. So we must be very careful about what we allow our eyes to see.

Psalms 119:36-37 Incline my heart unto thy testimonies, and not to covetousness. **Turn away mine eyes from beholding vanity;** and quicken thou me in thy way.

Again we see the word *vanity*, remember the definition of empty, worthless, having no value, substance or importance. God tells us not to let our eyes be looking at these types of things. It was looking at the wrong thing that brought about the very first sin of mankind.

Genesis 3:6 And when the woman saw that the tree was good for food, and **that it was pleasant to the eyes**, and a tree to be desired to make one wise, she took of the fruit thereof, and did eat, and gave also unto her husband with her; and he did eat.

God had given a very simple command. Yet, looking at the tree and listening to the wrong words caused the woman to forget God's command and to go by what her eyes lusted after.

Third: *The Pride of Life*. The word *pride* means, inordinate self esteem. God tells us that this life is not about us.

Revelation 4:11 Thou art worthy, O Lord, to receive glory and honour and power: for thou hast created all things, and **for thy pleasure** they are and were created.

People feel they are so important that the world needs to know their every move. They are proud of how many people put them on their friend list. They want the world to see them in their photos. Look at me! Listen to me! I have to post something every day. How can my friends make it if they don't hear from me today?

Proverbs 16:18 Pride goeth before destruction, and an haughty spirit before a fall.

God tells us that these things are not from Him, they are from the world and He tells us not to be friends with the world. Think about it very carefully, God judges us by our friendships. Look at your friendships and ask yourself, "What is God seeing in my friends?" Then understand that this is what He is seeing in you!

Ephesians 5:10-12 Proving what is acceptable unto the Lord. And have no fellowship with the unfruitful works of darkness, but rather reprove them. For it is a shame even to speak of those things which are done of them in secret.

CHAPTER 4

WRITE IT, REGRET IT!

I was watching a news report one day and they were talking about a murder case. The police had gone back and looked at the text that the suspect had sent out and the contacts on his computer. Reading through his notes they found many things that they were going to use as evidence against him. One of the lawyers made a very interesting statement. He said, "If you say it you can forget it but if you write it you will regret it."

As we are talking face to face with people, what is said in that specific conversation can be judged by the hearer so much differently than something that is printed. We can be joking around about something and it can be seen by the look on our face or by some gesture, (like a winking of the eye.) "He made me so mad; I wanted to kill him!" Both parties in the conversation know it was a joke, but what if it is written and someone is reading it that is not familiar with the background of the conversation? It could be taken the wrong way.

Many times a true statement can be turned into a lie. "I saw George kiss a woman that was not his wife." What have we learned from this statement? George is married. He is kissing someone he is not married to. This could look very bad for George. What a bum he must be. He is being unfaithful to his wife! I don't know George but I know this, I don't like guys that go around kissing women they are not married to. "Wait." Who is the woman that he kissed? It was his mom. Oh, well that is alright for a guy to give his mom a kiss. Now that we got the whole story the statement written takes on a whole new meaning.

Sadly, most people who write their little notes forget that everyone reading the note does not know everyone involved or do they know the circumstance of the discussion and many of these writings take on a wrong meaning. I have seen many families and friends have problems because of just one line that has been written. Often it spurs rebukes that create great battles that continue for a long time.

Anger in people often causes them to say things that they later regret. It is bad enough when you have a personal argument with one person but when hundreds get involved it can be like throwing a match into a pool of gas! Boom! The match might have caused a small burn between the two people or it could have easily been blown out by someone, but when it is thrown into the fuel, the fire then is hard to put out.

When you write things on these sites, even when you have deleted them, they will always be there in the memory of the computer and the memory of the web site. This should cause people to be very careful about what they write, because it can never be forgotten!

Psalms 39:1 I said, I will take heed to my ways, that I sin not with my tongue: I will keep my mouth with a bridle, while the wicked is before me.

This is wonderful advice from the Lord. We should pay close attention to the things that we say. We should keep our mouth with a bridle. The bridle is used to change the direction of the horse or to stop it. We should use a bridle to direct the words that we use or to stop ourselves from saying something that we will regret later.

James 1:26 If any man among you seem to be religious, and bridleth not his tongue, but deceiveth his own heart, this man's religion is vain.

He tells us plainly that our religion is empty if we do not learn to bridle our tongue. It is our communications that reveal what we really are on the inside. If we are to control all the other areas of our life, we must first learn to control how we communicate with others.

James 3:2-3 For in many things we offend all. If any man offend not in word, the same is a perfect man, and able also to bridle the whole body. Behold, we put bits in the horses' mouths, that they may obey us; and we turn about their whole body.

Thank the Lord, when we sin the Bible tells us that God will forgive us.

1 John 1:9 If we confess our sins, he is faithful and just to forgive us our sins, and to cleanse us from all unrighteousness.

Even better the Bible tells us that what is forgiven by God will never be remembered by Him.

Hebrews 10:17 And their sins and iniquities will I remember no more.

Psalms 103:12 As far as the east is from the west, so far hath he removed our transgressions from us.

Our sin and failure can be forgotten by God, but when we write it, the memory and perhaps the effects will be there for a long, long time!

CHAPTER 5

FACEBOOK ACCOUNTING

Matthew 12:34-37 O generation of vipers, how can ye, being evil, speak good things? for out of the abundance of the heart the mouth speaketh. A good man out of the good treasure of the heart bringeth forth good things: and an evil man out of the evil treasure bringeth forth evil things. But I say unto you, That **every idle word** that men shall speak, **they shall give account thereof in the day of judgment**. For by thy words thou shalt be justified, and by thy words thou shalt be condemned.

God warns us here that every idle word we use we will face someday at the judgment. The word "idle" means; trifling, useless, vain, and ineffectual. Sadly, much of what is communicated on these sites are just that, idle words. Words that is not important at all. Yet, many cannot go a day without reading them or writing them.

So many people are being hurt by words that are written. Abuse takes place every day. Though you may not say anything about someone, when you read it you become a part of it. The words will affect your attitude and your thoughts about those people who are being wronged.

There are even clubs that can be joined on these sites that the whole purpose is to hurt others. There is one that claims to be helping people who have been spiritually abused yet they abuse people themselves. Much of the abuse they write about is false, and then becomes abuse of the one they are accusing.

When you hear only one side of a story it is very often not totally correct. That is why in our court system there is a prosecution and a defense. If you only hear the prosecutor, it would be easy to find someone guilty. Many foolish people are writing things that could be proven totally false, yet people read it and accept it as a fact. This makes them just as foolish as the writer.

Sadly these foolish sites are being supported by millions of people.

Proverbs 26:4 Answer not a fool according to his folly, lest thou also be like unto him.

God warns that this kind of folly will always exist, but He also warns us not to participate in it. When we communicate with the fool, we encourage them to continue what they are doing we are adding fuel to the fire that is within them.

Everyone should realize that God keeps an account of what we say, what we hear, what we read and what we write. We will all give an account someday for this.

Think of all the feelings that you have as you read these post and see the photos. How does it affect your spirit and your attitude? How much time do you waste on these empty worthless things when right there close to you there is a Bible that is the written Word of Almighty God and you can't bring yourself to read it!

Proverbs 2:2-5 So that thou incline thine ear unto wisdom, and apply thine heart to understanding; Yea, if thou criest after knowledge, and liftest up thy voice for understanding; If thou seekest her as silver, and searchest for her as for hid treasures; Then shalt thou understand the fear of the LORD, and find the knowledge of God.

God has given us a great opportunity. We can search the Scripture, we can study to show ourselves approved unto God, we can hide His Word in our hearts to keep us from this sin, but it is not as important to many as what they read daily on their Facebook account! I do not want to stand before God someday and try to give an accounting for spending more time looking for the garbage of this world than I have seeking the treasures of His Holy Word.

Proverbs 10:19 In the multitude of words there wanteth not sin: but he that refraineth his lips is wise.

Again God is warning us that when there are too many words that the sin will also increase. Since we will be giving an account for every word we speak, every word we hear, every word we read and every word we write, this should cause each of us to be much more careful about our communications. All of our words are placed on our account! We will face each of these words on judgment day!

CHAPTER 6

THE FIRE OF HELL

James 3:4-6 Behold also the ships, which though they be so great, and are driven of fierce winds, yet are they turned about with a very small helm, whithersoever the governor listeth. Even so the tongue is a little member, and boasteth great things. Behold, how great a matter a little fire kindleth! And the tongue is a fire, a world of iniquity: so is the tongue among our members, that it defileth the whole body, and setteth on fire the course of nature; and it is set on **fire of hell.**

One match can start a fire that destroys a home just as one wrong statement can start a fire that can hurt a family or a friendship. In February of 2012 according to Facebook's recent S1 IPO Filing with the Securities and Exchange Commission, the site's users "generated an average of 2.7 billion Likes and Comments per day during the three months ended December 31, 2011." Break those numbers down, and it comes out to 112,500,000 Likes and Comments ever hour or about 1,875,000 every minute or, to break it down even further, around 31,250 Likes and Comments every second. Every day there are almost 3 billion statements being written or agreed to of this one web site. How many of them are negative or hurtful, we do not know. Yet, common sense will let us know that there are many of them that are creating problem for many people.

There are actually groups that can be found on these sites that their whole purpose is to spread discord. One such group is called "Spiritual Abuse Survivors." I understand that there are those who have been hurt. However, I know from personal experience that there are some that use this site have said things that are completely false and they themselves are doing the very thing they are supposed to be against. Many good people have had their names hurt by liars and what are even sadder are those who accept it. Why? Because it is written, so it must be true.

This is the fire of hell that God is talking of. Once the match has been lit, it is difficult to put out the fire or repair the damage that has already been done. Remember, it is not only the writers that are doing evil but also those that give ear to it.

Proverbs 26:20 Where no wood is, there the fire goeth out: so where there is no talebearer, the strife ceaseth.

If the match doesn't have anything to light, then the fire will not last long. The wood is the fuel for the fire and sites like Facebook are the fuel for these fires of hell.

Proverbs 17:4 A wicked doer giveth heed to false lips; and a liar giveth ear to a naughty tongue.

Notice, God's Word says that a wicked doer is one who listens to the one who is lying. Far too many Christians are fueling these fires and they don't even realize it. All of those that you support with your online friendships, you will one day give account to God for. They will have not only an effect on your judgment but they will have an effect on your personal life in the here and now.

Proverbs 13:20 He that walketh with wise men shall be wise: but **a companion of fools shall be destroyed.**

The word *Companion* means "One who keeps company with another." God' is very concerned with who our companions are. Notice it doesn't say that just the fool will be destroyed, but the companion. Are there any fools on your friend list? Are there any who are starting fires from hell? These are questions we should all pay attention to. Remember, everything you write and read on these sights is on record. Not just in some computer file but also in the books of Heaven.

Revelation 20:12 And I saw the dead, small and great, stand before God; and the books were opened: and another book was opened, which is the book of life: and the dead were judged out of those things which **were written in the books**, according to their works.

Ecclesiastes 12:14 For God shall bring every work into judgment, with every **secret thing,** whether it be good, or whether it be evil.

I cannot tell you all of the situations that I have had to deal with where something has been written and caused great pain to families. God's wisdom is so clear when it comes to communications and how we must be cautious in what we speak or hear. Also, it is very clear how subtly Satan works and uses something that can seem so innocent and simple to create problems that can never be fixed. Sadly, we cannot spiritually push a delete button and all the problems disappear.

We must realize that our tongue is a fire and a world of iniquity. It may be a small part of our body, but there is no doubt that it can do the greatest damage. Just as the bombs of today have powers that could not be imagined a hundred years ago, words today have powers that have multiplied millions of times because of the computer age.

Since our God was angry at the people who walked house to house carrying words of hell fire, how much more angry is He today because of people who can spread the fire around the world in just a moment? We should be more careful than ever as we carry our fire, realizing that there are all kinds of fuel for the fire all around us.

Proverbs 16:27 An ungodly man diggeth up evil: and in his lips there is as a burning fire.

CHAPTER 7

CYBER BUDDY & CYBER BULLY

Proverbs 1:10-16 My son, if sinners entice thee, consent thou not. If they say, Come with us, let us lay wait for blood, let us lurk privily for the innocent without cause: Let us swallow them up alive as the grave; and whole, as those that go down into the pit: We shall find all precious substance, we shall fill our houses with spoil: Cast in thy lot among us; let us all have one purse: My son, walk not thou in the way with them; refrain thy foot from their path: For their feet run to evil, and make haste to shed blood.

Here God warns us not to be enticed by the sinful of this world. Never before in history have the wicked of this world had the access to others as they do now. When I was a young man, to see a dirty movie, you had to go to the bad part of town to find a theater that would show that kind of dirt. So, if you were enticed to be a part of something like that you had to come up with a major plan of finding an excuse to be out at night. You had to find a way to get to the bad part of town and then disguise yourself so no one would recognize you. Today, all you have to do is push the wrong button on the computer and there it is.

Now, the wrong friend can entice you any minute of the day, when in the past they would have to actually make personal contact by coming to your home. Through today's technology they are with you everywhere you go as long as you have your phone or computer. In time past a friend had to meet the parents. If they came over or made a call the parents were more likely to be aware of what was happening. Now, there can be many relationships that the family is totally unaware of. People can block others from seeing what they are doing or they can create a false identity. The temptations to be involved in things that are wicked are now much more easily attained. Sadly, many believers are casting their lot in with the unbelievers and with the wicked.

Another warning from these verses is that there are those who want to hurt people for their own pleasure. This is what we call "bullying." Unfortunately, there have always been those who enjoy hurting others and picking on those that seems weaker. With today's technology this has become an even greater problem.

It is estimated that more than fifty percent of people on these sites have faced these kinds of attacks. It has also been determined that most young people will not tell their parents for fear of losing their access to these web sites. There are now "Cyber Bully" web sites where people can get information on how to deal with these problems.

How sad that we are inviting bullies into our homes. People are opening the door for their children to be tempted and to be hurt. Often in the news we hear of children who have taken their own lives because of what is being said about them on these sites. God has warned us not to walk in the way with them. Some will say "I don't bully people." Just know this that being involved with the bully makes you a part of the bullying.

I remember when I was a young child in school; there were times when I was being bullied by someone and every time there were people standing with the bully. They would not pick on me personally, but they would look and laugh. It seemed that their laughing hurt more than the bullying itself. To stand and watch someone hurt another and do nothing is a horrible thing. This is why God warns us over and again not to walk "with them." How many people are encouraging the bullies by being their buddies?

Psalms 50:18-22 When thou sawest a thief, then thou consentedst with him, and hast been partaker with adulterers. Thou givest thy mouth to evil, and thy tongue frameth deceit. Thou sittest and speakest against thy brother; thou slanderest thine own mother's son. These things hast thou done, and I kept silence; thou thoughtest that I was altogether such an one as thyself: but I will reprove thee, and set them in order before thine eyes. Now consider this, ye that forget God, lest I tear you in pieces, and there be none to deliver.

God is telling us that consenting to the sin is becoming a partaker of that sin! This is something everyone should consider when they are making these friendships.

Psalms 1:1 Blessed is the man that walketh not in the counsel of the ungodly, nor standeth in the way of sinners, nor sitteth in the seat of the scornful.

Proverbs 13:20 He that walketh with wise men shall be wise: but a companion of fools shall be destroyed.

We were going to hire you till
we checked out your Facebook site.
After we read some of your posts,
we realized that you are really stupid!!!

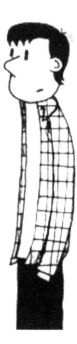

TWT

CHAPTER 8

USING WORDS AS A WEAPON

Psalms 64:2-4 Hide me from the secret counsel of the wicked; from the insurrection of the workers of iniquity: Who whet their tongue like a sword, and bend their bows to shoot their arrows, even bitter words: That they may shoot in secret at the perfect: suddenly do they shoot at him, and fear not.

When I was a child I was taught the little phrase, "Sticks and stones can break my bones but word will never hurt me." I have learned through the scripture and my life that this phrase is completely wrong! Words are some of the most painful things that I have dealt with in my life. I have seen many people hurt badly by what someone has said to them or about them.

Just as modern day weapons are more powerful than they were a hundred years ago, the modern day word weapon is much more powerful than ever. Hurtful words can be spread to the whole world in just moments. There are many people using their computers to take aim at people and to try and destroy their name and their lives.

God tells us that we should hide ourselves from these wicked people. They shoot out these words and have no fear of what their words will do to others. In fact many take great pleasure in bringing about this pain in people's lives.

Proverbs 30:14 There is a generation, whose teeth are as swords, and their jaw teeth as knives, to devour the poor from off the earth, and the needy from among men.

This verse fits our generation very well. Never before in history have people been able to use words to destroy others like they do today. Just as a person should be careful when they are handling a gun, they should be very careful with their words. Just like when you shoot a gun, you cannot grab the bullet out of the air once it is fired. Neither can we take back the words that we let go from our mouths or with our fingers typing them on our computer or our phone.

I remember a story that I was told as a child about a person who had went around his town saying evil things about a person. After he had done it, he felt bad and wanted to try and repair the damage that he had done. He went to a pastor and told him about the terrible mistake he had made and asked for advice on fixing the problem.

The preacher got a pillow and tore it open and gave the man a sack with many feathers from pillow. He then told him to go all over town to the houses that he had spread the evil story to and place a handful of feathers on the porch of that home. After he had gone to each home he then should return to the church and the pastor would then give him the next step in fixing the problem.

The man went and did as the pastor had told him and then he came back and asked him what he should do next. The pastor told him to go back to each home and collect all the feathers that he had laid down. The man replied that it was very windy that day and he was sure that all the feathers had blown away by now and that he could never find all of them, in fact he would be lucky if he could find any of them.

This showed him that once you put words out there, you can't take them back. The moral of the story was not to say things that are hurtful to people because once you have hurt them, you can't take away the pain.

James 3:6-8 And the tongue is a fire, a world of iniquity: so is the tongue among our members, that it defileth the whole body, and setteth on fire the course of nature; and it is set on fire of hell. For every kind of beasts, and of birds, and of serpents, and of things in the sea, is tamed, and hath been tamed of mankind: But the tongue can no man tame; it is an unruly evil, full of deadly poison.

God warns us that our tongues are full of deadly poison and that we must do all we can to control that deadly poison. Sadly, many today are doing just the opposite. They are purposefully using their computers and phones as a weapon.

Psalms 140:3 They have sharpened their tongues like a serpent; adders' poison is under their lips. Selah.

Ecclesiastes 10:11 Surely the serpent will bite without enchantment; and a babbler is no better.

With Facebook and other social media, those that are using these weapons have now become armies with many fellow soldiers who will help in the attacks. David in the book of Psalms tells us that he has been surrounded by people attacking him with their mouths.

Psalms 109:2-3 For the mouth of the wicked and the mouth of the deceitful are opened against me: they have spoken against me with a lying tongue. They compassed me about also with words of hatred; and fought against me without a cause.

Sadly this same thing is happening daily to millions of people who are being attacked with the weapon of words. We must always remember that the more powerful the weapon, the more careful we must be as we handle it. The technology of today has given each of us a more powerful weapon with our words than ever before. We must also remind ourselves that when involved in these types of activities, that all around us are others who are bearing the weapon of words and most of them are not being careful.

This puts us in a very dangerous position. It is almost like walking through the woods during hunting season wearing a deer outfit! There is a good chance you are going to get shot!

Psalms 52:1-5 Why boastest thou thyself in mischief, O mighty man? the goodness of God endureth continually. Thy tongue deviseth mischiefs; like a sharp razor, working deceitfully. Thou lovest evil more than good; and lying rather than to speak righteousness. Selah. Thou lovest all devouring words, O thou deceitful tongue. God shall likewise destroy thee for ever, he shall take thee away, and pluck thee out of thy dwelling place, and root thee out of the land of the living. Selah.

You had better work harder at being a good husband and watch every little word you say! If you don't, I'll tell it all on Twitter!
TWT

CHAPTER 9

FEEDING ON FOOLISHNESS

Proverbs 15:14 The heart of him that hath understanding seeketh knowledge: but the mouth of fools **feedeth on foolishness.**

There is so much good knowledge that is available to us today. There are many valuable lessons that all of us need to learn, especially from God's Word.

2 Peter 3:18 But grow in grace, and in the knowledge of our Lord and Saviour Jesus Christ. To him be glory both now and for ever. Amen.

We have the wonderful opportunity to get to know our Lord and Saviour better every day. We have access to God's Holy Word. We can listen to great men of God preach from God's Word. Thousands of wonderful books have been written that can teach us lessons that will change our lives for the better. There is so much wisdom that is available for us to feed on. Yet, many choose to feed themselves on the foolishness of this world.

In the Webster's 1828 Dictionary the word "foolish" is defined as: Void of understanding or sound judgment; weak in intellect; Unwise; imprudent; acting without judgment or discretion; silly; vain; trifling.

Again, God in His great wisdom describes to us what a fool gets involved in. He says that they feed on foolish things, things that are of no value. I recently saw a program where a man and his wife were seeking counsel from a famous talk show doctor. The wife was upset with the husband because he was spending over fifty hours a week on his computer communicating with friends on Facebook. The husband saw no problem with it but the wife was hurting terribly because she felt she was loosing the love of her husband.

Here we have an extreme case of a man who does not realize what he already has. He is willingly throwing it all away for the silly, vain, trifling thrill of communicating with others who have too much time on their hands. He has a wife who wants to spend time with him but the computer is more important. He was about to lose the love and relationship of his life for a bunch of empty relationships on a computer.

Many people are doing the same thing, just on a smaller level. They are missing out on their personal relationship with their family and with their God, just so they can feed on the foolishness found on their computer. There are many children in our churches today who have a very empty relationship with their parents. The parent will find time to text and to post on their computer but very little time teaching and training their children.

Proverbs 22:6 Train up a child in the way he should go: and when he is old, he will not depart from it.

Look at the definition of the word *train:* To exercise; to discipline; to teach and form by practice. God is telling us that if our children are to go the right way in life, the parents are going to have to take time and give great effort in seeing that they learn not only things in their mind, but also by practicing what they should do. Instead of being trained, they are put in front of a television, computer, or some electronic game.

How foolish is it for us to build relationships with people over the internet while the most valuable relationships we will ever possess are being ignored and thrown away.

The children of today are growing in the knowledge of the things in this world, but know very little about the proper relationship to God or their parents. Not only is this harmful spiritually, I believe that it hurts them mentally and physically. Not only do they need to have the spiritual and mental exercise, they also need the physical exercise. All of these if done properly are going to need the investment of more and more time.

Parents are now relying on drugs to control their children instead of doing the things that are needed to see them grow and learn. The Attention Deficit Disorder that they have may be from the fact that the parents are not paying attention to God and are paying too much attention to the things of this world! The Hyperactive Disorder they have may be that the parents are not active with them like they are with their computers.

Deuteronomy 6:6-7 And these words, which I command thee this day, shall be in thine heart: And thou shalt **teach them diligently** unto thy children, and shalt talk of them when thou **sittest** in thine house, and when thou **walkest** by the way, and when thou liest down, and when thou risest up.

We are told to teach "diligently." Notice when we are to teach. When we are sitting in the house, when we are outside walking, and when we go to bed and when we wake up. It is an all day job! It demands time and effort. I'm sorry! It won't be easy! From the moment they are born till they are grown, it will take effort!

How foolish is our generation? We are feeding on things of little or no value, while the eternal souls of our family are being forgotten.

Psalms 78:4-6 We will not hide them from their children, shewing to the generation to come the praises of the LORD, and his strength, and his wonderful works that he hath done. For he established a testimony in Jacob, and appointed a law in Israel, which he commanded our fathers, that they should make them known to their children: That the generation to come might know them, even the children which should be born; who should arise and declare them to their children:

Many parents are showing their children that only the petty things of this world are what is important and not the eternal things of God. I have had children tell me that they can't communicate with their mom because she is always on the computer. She is so focused on herself and her Facebook friends that she cannot even look into the face of her child and have a good, long, godly conversation with them. A conversation that could make a wonderful difference in the child's life and also give them a memory that would last beyond the parent's life. Sadly, that child will have the memory that mom is more interested in computer friends than she is in her child. Then when some wrong person finally does pay them some attention, they are likely to follow that person and many times where they follow them can turn out tragic!

Not only does feeding on these foolish things hurt the parent and child relationship, it is also destroying many marriages. Remember the vows taken at the wedding? I will love, honor and cherish you! I will forsake all others and remain faithful as long as we both shall live.

Far too many are more faithful to their Facebook friends than they are to their mate. Just as raising good children takes time and effort, building a good marriage takes time and effort. If you are to be the best parents you must work at being good mates! Loving each other and living for each other will give your home a stronger foundation.

The wise man builds his house upon the rock!

Matthew 7:24 Therefore whosoever heareth these sayings of mine, and doeth them, I will liken him unto a wise man, which built his house upon a rock:

Notice that God tells us that the rock our foundation comes from hearing what He says and then doing it! God in His word gives us very clear instructions on what to do and what not to do.

Ephesians 5:25 Husbands, love your wives, even as Christ also loved the church, and gave himself for it;

Titus 2:4 That they may teach the young women to be sober, to love their husbands, to love their children,

God wants us to love our mate and to love and train our children. We are warned over and again to stop feeding on the foolish things of this world and to focus on the eternal.

CHAPTER 10

MEDDLERS

Proverbs 20:3 It is an honour for a man to cease from strife: but **every fool will be meddling.**

Proverbs 20:19 He that goeth about as a talebearer revealeth secrets: **therefore meddle not with him** that flattereth with his lips.

We can learn so much from looking at the definition of words. The word I want us to look at now is the word, *meddle* or *meddler*. This means; to have to do; to take part; to interpose and act in the concerns of others, or in affairs in which one's interposition is not necessary; often with the sense of intrusion; to mix, to mingle; one that interferes or busies himself with things in which he has no concern; a busy body.

God is clearly telling us that one of the main characteristics of a fool is that they feel they must be involved in the affairs of other people. Many Christians are spending hours every day looking into the lives of other people and they also put things online that draw others into the field of meddlers.

We are not to take part in things that are not our business. We are not supposed to mix and mingle with others who are involved in things that really don't matter. Satan has hooked people into getting so involved in these sites and in the lives of their friends that they are not paying the proper attention to the things and the people that really do matter.

Every husband and wife should be focused on the relationship with their mate. Spending face to face time is so much better than Facebook time. God wants married couples to have close and intimate relationships. A proper love relationship brings great contentment to our lives.

Proverbs 31:10-12 Who can find a virtuous woman? for her price is far above rubies. The heart of her husband doth safely trust in her, so that he shall have no need of spoil. She will do him good and not evil all the days of her life.

Hebrews 13:4 Marriage is honourable in all, and the bed undefiled: but whoremongers and adulterers God will judge.

Ephesians 5:25 Husbands, love your wives, even as Christ also loved the church, and gave himself for it;

In my many years of marriage counseling, I have seen that one of the big problems in homes is the lack of good communication and proper love relationships.

Sadly, with the new world of electronic communication, the world of good personal communication has almost ceased to exist in many homes. When men and women should be focusing on each other they are now looking into the lives of their many Facebook friends and their texting partners.

Another area of focus in our lives should be our relationship with our children.

To have a proper relationship with a child a parent must spend many hours communicating personally with them.

Deuteronomy 6:6-9 And these words, which I command thee this day, shall be in thine heart: And thou shalt teach them diligently unto thy children, and shalt talk of them when thou sittest in thine house, and when thou walkest by the way, and when thou liest down, and when thou risest up. And thou shalt bind them for a sign upon thine hand, and they shall be as frontlets between thine eyes. And thou shalt write them upon the posts of thy house, and on thy gates.

Notice that God wants the parent to be diligent in their communication with their children. We are told to teach them and to talk with them during every part of the day!

No, this will not be easy! It is much easier to set them in front of the TV or computer and let them learn their lessons from the world than it is to take the time to focus our lives on them. Sadly, many children grow up not really knowing their parents. Even sadder is that many parents see their kids grow up and walk away and they really don't know their child.

No wonder God tells us that those who focus on meddling are fools. They are throwing away their greatest treasures to take part in things that are of no value at all.

There is another area that I believe Christians should be focused on. That is their relationship with God and their church. There is no doubt that God wants to have a close personal relationship with each of us. If you are not saved, God wants to save you right now! Not just so you can go to heaven when you die but so He can have a close, personal relationship with you right now.

He also makes you part of a church for His purpose. God compares the church to a body. Just as our human body has many different parts that must function correctly for us to be physically healthy, our church needs all of it's parts to be doing what they need to be doing for the church to be spiritually healthy. Many churches today are struggling because many of their parts are not doing the works that God had intended.

How wonderful it would be if people were as faithful and focused on their work for the Lord as they are on their computer sites. It is not easy to do the right things.

Matthew 7:13-14 Enter ye in at the strait gate: for wide is the gate, and broad is the way, that leadeth to destruction, and many there be which go in thereat: Because strait is the gate, and narrow is the way, which leadeth unto life, and few there be that find it.

God has told us that the easy way is the way to destruction. The ways that lead to life are strait and narrow. This means that it is not an easy path. Notice that He says that *"few people find it."* This tells me that we must be focused and looking if we are going to stay on the right path of life. Through my many years of pastoring I have seen many people go down the wrong path. The path always starts off easy but it always ends in destruction. I have also watched those who focus on God, the Bible, their church and their family work hard at staying on that right path and the end has always been good!

The foolish meddlers are too focused on the here and now and what brings them immediate pleasure while those with wisdom look beyond this life to things of eternal value.

CHAPTER 11

CREEP INTO HOUSES

2 Timothy 3:1-7 This know also, that in the last days perilous times shall come. For men shall be lovers of their own selves, covetous, boasters, proud, blasphemers, disobedient to parents, unthankful, unholy, Without natural affection, trucebreakers, false accusers, incontinent, fierce, despisers of those that are good, Traitors, heady, highminded, lovers of pleasures more than lovers of God; Having a form of godliness, but denying the power thereof: from such turn away. For of this sort are they which creep into houses, and lead captive silly women laden with sins, led away with divers lusts, Ever learning, and never able to come to the knowledge of the truth.

In these verses God is warning us of the attitude of the world in the last days. He tells us that it will be a very perilous time. The word *perilous* is defined as; Dangerous; hazardous; full of risk; exposure of person or property to injury.

I believe we are living in those "last days." I believe that never before have people been more exposed than they are right now. We can go online and see so much of what is going on in a person's life. People are willingly opening up their lives for the world to see. This fits well with the first phrase in verse two. Men shall be lovers of their own selves.

God then gives a long list of the evil that will be taking place in the hearts and lives of those that are in love with themselves. He then tells us that when we see this kind of attitude and spirit that we should turn away from it. He knows that if we don't, it will become our spirit and our attitude.

What I want us to look at now is what God says to us in verse six.

For of this sort are they which **creep into houses**, and **lead captive silly women** laden with sins, led away with divers lusts,

I know that this verse is very offensive to some. Before you get offended let us look at the definitions of two words. The word "*creep;*" This means to move secretly; to move as to escape detection, or prevent suspicion. God is warning us that if we are not very careful these rotten spirits will sneak into our homes. Many will not realize it till it is too late.

Imagine how you would feel to wake up in the middle of the night and see a stranger standing at the foot of your bed with a knife in his hand. When you see him you will know immediately that it is not for good. You didn't hear as he picked the lock on your back door. You didn't pay attention as your dog barked as he slowly made his way through your house. How did he know that you would be alone this night? He is here right now, you are not prepared to defend yourself and now something horrible happens.

After all is done you think of ways you could have been better prepared but sadly it is too late! This is much like what is happening with the new technology that we have in this world. There are many bad things moving secretly into people's lives, yet when they finally realize what has happened, it may be too late.

God tells us that we need to be alert. We need to have some alarm systems in our hearts and lives that will alert us when these evils make their moves. Just as the criminal will not call and give you warning that he is coming to rob your house, Satan will not warn you that he is out to destroy your home and your life. He is going to "creep in!"

The next word I want to look at is the word *"silly,"* This means weak in intellect; foolish; witless; destitute of ordinary strength of mind; simple. No one ever wants to admit that they can be fooled easily by someone. The truth is that everyone can be "lead captive" by someone.

We must always remember that Satan has been about his business for thousands of years. He has taken advantage of nearly everyone at some point in life. Throughout the Bible we see where some of the greatest men of faith have been lead astray by the wiles of the devil.

Never in the history of the world has Satan had such easy access into people houses as he does today. He is creeping into houses through the news papers, magazines, radio, television, telephones, cell phones, computers, and many other modern devices that lead people away from what is good and right to those things that are wasteful and worthless.

We need to wake up to the barking that is being heard all around us. There are warnings coming out every day showing us that Satan is using these new web tools to creep into our homes and lives! This book is a good alarm system for each of you to use but the best alarm system you can have is Jesus as you Saviour, the Holy Bible as your guide book and the Holy Spirit to help guard your life.

We all need protection from Satan. The Bible tells us that he can transform himself into an angel of light. He disguises himself in many ways. So, we must be sober and vigilant because he wants to devour and destroy our lives. No matter how smart you are, compared to Satan you are simple and your only hope is to listen to the only one who can help you and that is the Lord our God!

2 Corinthians 11:14 And no marvel; for Satan himself is transformed into an angel of light.

1 Peter 5:8 Be sober, be vigilant; because your adversary the devil, as a roaring lion, walketh about, seeking whom he may devour:

CHAPTER 12

FORESEEING THE EVIL

Proverbs 22:3 A prudent man foreseeth the evil, and hideth himself: but the simple pass on, and are punished.

The word *prudent* in the Webster's 1828 dictionary is defines as; Cautious; circumspect; practically wise; careful of the consequences of enterprises, measures or actions; cautious not to act when the end is of doubtful utility.

God is telling us that we need to have the wisdom to consider the possible outcomes of things we are getting involved in. In our day and time, new things are coming out nearly every day. Things have changed so much in the past few decades.

These new means of communication are opening doors that we have never been through before. Millions of people are walking through these doors without stopping to think much about what might be on the other side of the door. It's a new door into a new world that is bringing about new problems.

If you pay attention to the news, we are beginning to hear more and more about the things that are on the other side of that door. Every week we are hearing new stories of the terrible things that are coming about because of these new methods of communication.

God is very gracious and He warns us of these evils. Yet many pay little or no attention to these warnings, much like the people of Egypt in the time of Moses. God had been sending many plagues upon Egypt and now He was about to send a fiery hail. He even tells them when it is coming, but many people paid no attention.

Exodus 9:20-21 He that feared the word of the LORD among the servants of Pharaoh made his servants and his cattle flee into the houses: And he that regarded not the word of the LORD left his servants and his cattle in the field.

Another good example of someone foreseeing evil was Noah. He heard God's warning and began to build the ark. He respected God and he loved his family so much that he built a giant boat that was no where near water. He must have been looked at like he was crazy by his neighbors, yet he continued for years building the ark.

Hebrews 11:7 By faith Noah, being warned of God **of things not seen as yet**, moved with fear, prepared an ark to the saving of his house; by the which he condemned the world, and became heir of the righteousness which is by faith.

He saved his family because he listened to the warning from God. Imagine the fear upon all those around the ark as the rain began to fall and the floods began to rise.

The door was shut; they could not get in the ark. They failed to listen to the warnings.

Proverbs 14:16 A wise man feareth, and departeth from evil: but the fool rageth, and is confident.

Many today who will not pay attention to God's warnings about evil communications will one day find they are facing the consequences. The problem is that when people recognize the problem it is too late to stop the problem. The damages are done!

Yes, there is forgiveness of sin, but sadly the scars remain. No wonder God repeats himself from Proverbs 22:3

Proverbs 27:12 A prudent man foreseeth the evil, and hideth himself; but the simple pass on, and are punished.

We need to be cautious with all of this new technology. We need to look at the possible problems that can come from them. God tells us to hide ourselves from these things. We should not be as the fool who is so confident in his own judgment that he will ignore the warnings of God.

Proverbs 3:7 Be not wise in thine own eyes: fear the LORD, and depart from evil.

We must understand that when God gave us His Word; He saw the future. He knew that one day there would be computers and cell phones. In His great wisdom He gave us warnings that our ears and hearts should be open to. We should be able to foresee the evil. Actually, we are now seeing the evil right before our eyes. Yet, many are not going to pay attention to what they are seeing. They will be like the young man God tells us about who had no understanding and the fool that was so full of words that he could be taught nothing.

Proverbs 7:7 And beheld among the simple ones, I discerned among the youths, a young man void of understanding,

Proverbs 7:22-24 He goeth after her straightway, as an ox goeth to the slaughter, or as a fool to the correction of the stocks; Till a dart strike through his liver; as a bird hasteth to the snare, and knoweth not that it is for his life. Hearken unto me now therefore, O ye children, and attend to the words of my mouth.

Ecclesiastes 10:12-14 The words of a wise man's mouth are gracious; but the lips of a fool will swallow up himself. The beginning of the words of his mouth is foolishness: and the end of his talk is mischievous madness. A fool also **is full of words**: a man cannot tell what shall be; and what shall be after him, **who can tell him?**

Many are so in love with what they are doing that they do not want to hear the truth. They do not like the rebuke of God's word and God's wisdom. They would rather believe a lie than to learn the truth. God describes this attitude in the Book of Isaiah.

Isaiah 30:9-10 That this is a rebellious people, lying children, children that will not hear the law of the LORD: Which say to the seers, See not; and to the prophets, Prophesy not unto us right things, speak unto us smooth things, prophesy deceits:

If you have read this far, I hope you see how much scripture is being used. I hope you can look beyond the moments of pleasure that you get from social media and recognize the danger and destruction that are ahead. Just as we should recognize that our Lord will come soon and His judgment will come also, we must understand that there will be a price to pay for being involved in things that are wicked.

1 Thessalonians 5:6-8 Therefore let us not sleep, as do others; but let us watch and be sober. For they that sleep sleep in the night; and they that be drunken are drunken in the night. But let us, who are of the day, be sober, putting on the breastplate of faith and love; and for an helmet, the hope of salvation.

CHAPTER 13

WHAT WE TAKE PART IN REVEALS WHO WE ARE

Proverbs 17:4 A wicked doer giveth heed to false lips; and a liar giveth ear to a naughty tongue.

God tells us that it is not just what we do that reveals our character but also what we listen and pay attention to. Many do not realize that in the eyes of God, you are what you take part in. Giving heed to lies makes you wicked. Hearing naughty things makes you a liar.

Proverbs 28:4 They that forsake the law praise the wicked: but such as keep the law contend with them.

Have you considered who your Facebook friends are? Do you realize that your name on their friends list is showing your approval of them? Being one of their numbers is giving them praise. How many people are taking part in something that they do not even realize they are a part of? Earlier in the book I made the statement; "You are now or soon shall be what your friends are." This is a truth of God's Word. God will judge us by our friendships.

This should wake you up! You will give account to God not only for your doings but God will judge us for the things we approve of in our friends.

Romans 1:32 Who knowing the judgment of God, that they which commit such things are worthy of death, not only do the same, but have pleasure in them that do them.

God is telling us that enjoying the sin of others makes us as worthy of judgment as those that are doing the sin. I don't know about you but dealing with my own sin and my own faults is scary enough for me! When we stand before God someday for many it will be like facing a credit card bill after we have given our credit card number to all of our friends and then at the end of the month having to pay the bill for all that they have charged.

Can you imagine how big that bill would be and can you imagine what they would be using your number for? Just as we protect our bank account and our credit accounts, we should definitely protect our accounting to God.

Proverbs 17:15 He that justifieth the wicked, and he that condemneth the just, even they both are abomination to the LORD.

The word "justify" means to accept as just and to treat with favor, to pardon and clear from guilt. God is telling us clearly that this is an abomination to Him. When you accept those that are doing these wicked things on your friends list, this angers God! How can those who love God and His Word give our approval to those who are doing wicked things?

Psalms 10:2-4 The wicked in his pride doth persecute the poor: let them be taken in the devices that they have imagined. For the wicked boasteth of his heart's desire, and blesseth the covetous, whom the LORD abhorreth. The wicked, through the pride of his countenance, will not seek after God: **God is not in all his thoughts**.

How few people on these sites are thinking of God? God tells us that the wicked are thinking of their self. Pride is their focus. The

59

word wicked is defined as: To decline, to err, to deviate, also to fold; Evil in principle or practice; deviating from divine law.

Looking at this definition should awaken many to realize that they are not only fellowshipping with the wicked but they themselves are becoming one of the wicked.

Many will be shocked come judgment day when God has them give account for things they did not even realize they were a part of.

Ecclesiastes 11:9 Rejoice, O young man, in thy youth; and let thy heart cheer thee in the days of thy youth, and walk in the ways of thine heart, and in the sight of thine eyes: but know thou, that for all these things **God will bring thee into judgment.**

Ecclesiastes 12:13-14 Let us hear the conclusion of the whole matter: Fear God, and keep his commandments: for this is the whole duty of man. For **God shall bring every work into judgment**, with every secret thing, whether it be good, or whether it be evil.

2 Corinthians 5:10 For **we must all appear before the judgment seat of Christ**; that every one may receive the things done in his body, according to that he hath done, whether it be good or bad.

God very clearly tells us that He looks at our relationship with this world and the things of this world to determine our relationship with Him.

James 4:4 Ye adulterers and adulteresses, know ye not that the friendship of the world is enmity with God? whosoever **therefore will be a friend of the world is the enemy of God**.

If our friendship is with the world then we have made God our enemy! I don't know about you, but I want God on my side, I want to be on His side. Jesus tells us how we can be His friend.

John 15:14 Ye are my friends, if ye do whatsoever I command you.

Matthew 12:50 For whosoever shall do the will of my Father which is in heaven, the same is my brother, and sister, and mother.

If there is a friend that we all should seek, it is Jesus! If there is approval that we are seeking, it should be from Jesus! If there is someone we should be committed to, it is Jesus! We must always remember that what we take part in is the revealer of who we really are! What we spend our time involved in shows us what we really love!

Our daughter moved to Florida, got married and has just had a baby boy that she named after you!!! We need to check her Facebook page more often!

TWT

CHAPTER 14

POURING OUT FOOLISHNESS

Proverbs 15:1-2 A soft answer turneth away wrath: but grievous words stir up anger. The tongue of the wise useth knowledge aright: but the mouth of fools **poureth out foolishness.**

Communication is a wonderful gift from God. It is a way to share our faith in God, and our love for our family and friends. We can use it to protect those we love by warning them of the dangers around them. Communication is great when it is good communication however when it is used in a foolish way, it can create great problems and it takes away from the good communication.

God tells us that the tongue of the wise uses their communication skills in a right manor. They are careful about the words that come from their mouth. They understand that some things are better left unsaid.

Proverbs 29:20 Seest thou a man that is **hasty in his words**? there is more hope of a fool than of him.

We have heard the phrase "speaking without thinking." This is something that is a greater danger today than ever before. A person reads or hears something and before they know the whole story, they respond. Now it is too late! You have spoken your mind and your mind was wrong. God tells us that there is more hope of a fool than the one who is quick to speak their mind.

James 1:19 Wherefore, my beloved brethren, let every man be swift to hear, **slow to speak,** slow to wrath:

Proverbs 17:28 Even a fool, when he holdeth his peace, is counted wise: and he that **shutteth his lips** is esteemed a man of understanding.

Sadly, there are many today who feel it necessary to say everything that comes into their mind. God tells us that the mouth of the fool pours out foolish things. Things that are valueless and empty. They are communicating about things that are of no value.

What most don't realize is that this worthless communication ends up destroying valuable communication. I have heard how many people put others on their phone reject list because they are sick and tired of the constant and worthless messages that they receive.

Many people communicate only by texting because they hate the thought of having what they consider a worthless conversation with someone. The foolish communication is rampant in our world today. When there is nothing to say people feel they have to say something. They cannot go a day without posting a note. How can their friends survive the day if they don't know that they are awake, have had their bath, have eaten their breakfast and are now watching the morning news! There, now the world can go on because I am awake, I have made my daily post or should I say my hourly post or perhaps my every five minute post!

How nice it used to be when you would go to the mail box and get a letter from someone you loved. You know that they had actually taken time to set down and think about you and to communicate only with you. It was special because it wasn't something hasty and empty. It wasn't written in some weird short handed abbreviation type writing.

It was hand written, placed in an envelope, sealed, stamped and then mailed. When it arrived at your home you knew that it meant something. Thirty three years ago I lived far away from my fiancé, who is now my wife. I still have the letters that were written to me from her. They meant a lot to me then and they still mean a lot to me today!

It was not worthless communication. There was a purpose behind our communicating. On the days when I could call and talk to her, I was thrilled and when the time came when I could actually see her face to face, it meant so much to me.

God is for proper communication, and so I am for proper communication. The foolish, worthless, empty communications that are going on so rampantly today is against God, and His purpose for giving us the ability to communicate.

Read in the Bible the story of the Tower of Babel. The whole earth was of one language and they were using their communications to go against God and His plan.

Genesis 11:6-7 And the LORD said, Behold, the people is one, and they have all one language; and this they begin to do: and now nothing will be restrained from them, which they have imagined to do. Go to, let us go down, and there confound their language, that they may not understand one another's speech.

Notice that God chose to disrupt their communications. He scattered them all over the world and gave them different languages. This kept them from doing the things that they had imagined in their hearts to do.

We need to understand that proper communication is a wonderful thing. When it is used wisely it can accomplish much for God and our families.

Isaiah 50:4 The Lord GOD hath given me the tongue of the learned, that I should know how to speak a word in season to him that is weary: he wakeneth morning by morning, he wakeneth mine ear to hear as the learned.

Like Isaiah, we should desire to have a learned tongue; we should know how to speak and when to speak. We should understand the value of proper communications.

Proverbs 25:11 A word fitly spoken is like apples of gold in pictures of silver.

Proverbs 15:23 A man hath joy by the answer of his mouth: and a word spoken in due season, how good is it!

We can teach our children things that will last them a lifetime. We can share with them the truths of the Word of God. We can teach them about life, and how to work. We can make wonderful memories with them that they can carry with them forever. This is valuable communications. It is not pouring out foolishness.

Son, why didn't you text
me goodnight???

CHAPTER 15

DELIVERY FROM DANGER

Proverbs 2:16 To deliver thee from the strange woman, even from the stranger which flattereth with her words;

Proverbs 6:24 To keep thee from the evil woman, from the flattery of the tongue of a strange woman.

In the book of Proverbs it is a father giving his son warnings and advice about life. Here he warns his son about having conversations with a stranger. The father knew that there were people in the world that would try to take advantage of his child.

There are many people who will be friendly with the ultimate goal of using that friendship for their own personal gain. We have heard many stories in the news of cases of adultery and fornication that have come about through the friendships made on the computer. Many people are getting in touch with boyfriends or girlfriends from their past and restoring the old flames that once burned and in doing so burn up their present marriage.

We hear of perverts and pedophiles that get to know children on these sites and then commit horrible acts of abuse. These are dangers that have always been out there but now it is much different. Through the social media, people are inviting these dangers directly into their homes.

God warns His children to stay away from those who, through flattering words can convince you to do something that had it not been for your communication with them, it would have never happened.

Another danger that many are unaware of is the danger of becoming the "strange person." In other words becoming the one who entices another to do something they should not do. There are things inside of most people that would never come out. However, when tempted day after day and seeing others do what their mind has thought of, they have a greater likelihood of saying or doing something online that they could never bring themselves to do if this avenue of cyber space had not been opened to them.

God warns us that we are all capable of sin. Therefore, we must have standards and restrictions in our own lives that will help keep us from falling.

Galatians 6:1 Brethren, if a man be overtaken in a fault, ye which are spiritual, restore such an one in the spirit of meekness; considering thyself, **lest thou also be tempted.**

Colossians 3:5-8 **Mortify** therefore your members which are upon the earth; fornication, uncleanness, inordinate affection, evil concupiscence, and covetousness, which is idolatry: For which things' sake the wrath of God cometh on the children of disobedience: In the which ye also walked some time, when ye lived in them. But now ye also put off all these; anger, wrath, malice, blasphemy, **filthy communication out of your mouth.**

God warn us that even if we are a spiritual person, we must be careful when helping others. He tells us to mortify our members. The word "mortify" means {to subdue, to abase, to humble, to restrain, to bring into subjection} we must recognize our own personal weakness, if we don't we are likely to fall into sin.

I have been saved since 1966; I surrendered my life to preach in 1975, I have been married since 1980, I have raised 5 children, I love the Lord, I love the Bible, I love my wife and family with all my heart. Though I believe that I will never go back on any of my commitments, I am still very cautious in every area of my life.

I have seen it multiple times over the years. When a man starts thinking he is incapable of sin and failure, he lets down his guard and the next thing you know, and he has fallen. These falls are great victories for our enemy!

Zechariah 11:2 Howl, fir tree; for the cedar is fallen; because the mighty are spoiled: howl, O ye oaks of Bashan; for the forest of the vintage is come down.

In this verse God tells the small fir tree to cry out because the large cedar has fallen. What is being pictured here is a giant tree being cut down and as it falls it crushes many little trees that are around it. God is letting us know that if we fall we will hurt those who look up to and respect us. Our falling will cause them to fall also.

We all are cedars to someone. We are all fir trees to someone. We must understand that the danger we put ourselves in, can ultimately hurt, not only us, but many around us.

Proverbs 7:21-23 With her **much fair speech** she caused him to yield, with the flattering of her lips **she forced him**. He goeth after her straightway, as an ox goeth to the slaughter, or as a fool to the correction of the stocks; Till a dart strike through his liver; as a bird hasteth to the snare, and **knoweth not that it is for his life.**

God compares a woman seducing a man with her word to rape. "She forced him" the Bible says. How did she force him? She forced him with her words. He thought he had been convinced to have a good time but what he had been convinced of was destroying his whole life.

God through His Word is trying to deliver people from danger. Sadly, these communication sites are to them like this fair and beautiful woman. They cannot resist what she is offering. They do not see it but they are being spiritually raped. They are being lead to the slaughter, but they don't know it. Sadly, many will not realize it till it is too late!

Proverbs 7:22 He goeth after her straightway, as an ox goeth to the slaughter, or as a fool to the correction of the stocks;

Proverbs 9:16-18 Whoso is simple, let him turn in hither: and as for him that wanteth understanding, she saith to him, Stolen waters are sweet, and bread eaten in secret is pleasant. But he knoweth not that the dead are there; and that her guests are in the **depths of hell.**

It should be the prayer of everyone, that God would protect us from the dangers of this world. We must always remember the importance of not putting ourselves into dangerous situations as many of God's people are doing in the name of pleasure.

Psalms 39:8 **Deliver me** from **all my transgressions**: make me not the reproach of the foolish.

Psalms 59:2 **Deliver me** from the workers of iniquity, and save me from bloody men.

CHAPTER 16

FILTHY COMMUNICATION

Colossians 3:8 But now ye also put off all these; anger, wrath, malice, blasphemy, **filthy communication out of your mouth.**

Again we will go to the Webster's 1828 Dictionary to look at the definitions of some words. First the word "*filthy*": [Dirty; foul; unclean; nasty; polluted; defiled by sinful practices; morally impure; obtained by base and dishonest means.] The next definition I want to look at is for the word "*communication*": [the act of imparting, conferring, or delivering from one to another; as the communication of knowledge, opinions or facts; Intercourse by words, letters or messages; interchange of thoughts or opinions, by conference or other means.]

God in His great wisdom and foresight saw that the world of communication would constantly be changing. We now have many other means of sharing our words and our thoughts. This can be a wonderful thing if the communication is clean. Yet, when it is filthy, like much of what is being shared today, a person must learn to be very careful about the communication they give and receive.

We live in a time where many people have become very conscience of the spreading of germs. All over the country, when you enter or exit businesses you see dispensers that you can put your hand under and you will have some kind of germ killer sprayed on your hand. The fear of the microscopic germs that might be on the cart you are pushing cause you to be cautious.

Sadly people are not being cautious about the germs that are being spread through the filthy communication on the phones and computers.

2 Peter 2:7-8 And delivered just Lot, vexed with the filthy conversation of the wicked: (For that righteous man dwelling among them, in seeing and hearing, vexed his righteous soul from day to day with their unlawful deeds;)

Here we see one of the very sad stories in the Bible of a man who ends up losing part of his family and then disgracing himself with others in his family. It came about not because of what he himself was doing but because of what he saw around him. The Bible tells us that he was a righteous man. However, what he saw and heard from the filthy conversation of the wicked started him down the path that led to the destruction.

If he had looked ahead and saw what moving to this area would do to his family, I believe he would have chosen to stay in the wilderness and have a relationship with God over living a life of ease in this wicked city.

Two of his daughters married wrong and ended up dying with their families in the destruction of Sodom. He and his other family members had to leave in a hurry losing all the properties that they had been living in and for. His wife was turned to a pillar of salt when she looked back. Later his other daughters got him drunk and had sex with their own dad, this to me being the lowest moment of all!

Remember, God tells us that this all came out for Lot because of the filthy conversation of the wicked.

There are many Christians today who like Lot are not recognizing the filth that they are allowing into their lives through these worldly web sites. They don't see the things that may be infecting their children or their own lives.

I have already seen how many lives have been affected by the filthy communication of the world. I don't believe we have seen even the tip of the iceberg yet! Right now, I feel we are just in the sowing stage. In the years to come we will begin to see the harvest in many people's lives.

When I think of Lot and his family, I imagine that when they left the wilderness to live in the city, it must have felt pretty good, especially for the mother. It had to be very difficult to constantly be moving, living in a tent. Life for her probably seemed much simpler.

How heart breaking it must have been as they left the city, told by God not to look back! But, she had children still in that town, her home was there! When the fire and brimstone began to fall and the cry of the city was heard, her girls were there, her son's in law were there maybe even some grandchildren. She could not stop herself from looking back! Too bad they hadn't looked ahead! They did not foresee the evil that was coming.

I am very afraid that many families are doing something very similar today! The ease of communication today feels pretty good but they fail to pay attention to the filth that they are exposing themselves and their families to. I have no doubt that there will be many who years from now, like Mrs. Lot, will be looking back wishing that they had taken time to look ahead and recognize the dangers.

Colossians 3:7-9 In the which ye also walked some time, when ye lived in them. But now ye also put off all these; anger, wrath, malice, blasphemy, filthy communication out of your mouth. Lie not one to another, seeing that ye have put off the old man with his deeds;

Proverbs 19:27 Cease, my son, to hear the instruction that causeth to err from the words of knowledge.

CHAPTER 17

THE CONGREGATION OF EVIL DOERS

Psalms 26:4-5 I have not sat with vain persons, neither will I go in with dissemblers. I have hated the congregation of evil doers; and will not sit with the wicked.

The wisdom and foresight of our God never ceases to amaze me. The Bible tells us that every word of God is pure and that His words are a shield to us.

Proverbs 30:5 Every word of God is pure: he is a shield unto them that put their trust in him.

In this chapter's opening verse we see some very important words. When we look at the definition of those words, we see some great lessons that should encourage people to be very careful about their online and on phone relationships with people.

Once again we see God use the word "*vain*." Remember that this word means: Empty, worthless, no substance, value or importance. We are told that we should not sit with these kinds of people. Even more important we should not be one of these people.

The next word we should see in this verse is the word "dissemblers." The definition of this word is very fitting with today's society of online and on phone communicators. The definition of this word is: To be hypocritical; to assume a false appearance; to conceal the real fact, motive, intention or sentiments under some pretence.

This definition is a message in itself. For those involved in these types of communication, you know that there are many who do each of these things on a daily or should I say on an hourly basis. We are warned not to be a part of this kind of a group. I have mentioned it before, but it needs to be said again, "You are now or soon shall be what your friends are!" Don't sit with them, don't go with them!

If we are to have a proper relationship with God, we must separate ourselves from those things that our God is against.

2 Corinthians 6:17-18 Wherefore **come out from among them**, and be ye separate, saith the Lord, and touch not the unclean thing; and I will receive you, And will be a Father unto you, and ye shall be my sons and daughters, saith the Lord Almighty.

Far too many people are more focused on having a relationship with the wrong kind of people than having a close and intimate relationship with our Heavenly Father.

The next word I want us to look at is the word, congregation. The word congregation's definition is; the act of bringing together, or assembling. The other word is evil. This word is defined as having a bad quality of a natural kind; mischievous; having qualities that tend to injury, or produce mischief. The second definition of evil is also important; having a bad quality of a moral kind; wicked; corrupt; perverse; wrong.

God is telling us that this kind of congregation should be hated! This is not a group that God's people should be associated with. Look up the foundation of Facebook and you will see that it was started with an evil purpose in mind.

Back when it started the founder was a student at Harvard University and he had a site called "Facemash," a hot or not clone for Harvard. It would place photos of girls on the site and have people vote to rank them according to their looks. This was not done with the people's permission. It was so bad that even on the Harvard campus this man was brought before a disciplinary board. According to a November 19, 2003, Harvard Crimson article, he was charged with breaching security, violating copyrights, and violating individual privacy.

This fits the definition of evil! These kinds of things are happening every moment of every day on these kinds of communication sites. Anyone who has been involved in these has probably seen these things happen. We are told to hate these kinds of gathering places.

The last phrase in the opening verse of this chapter says that we should not sit with the wicked. The word *wicked* means; evil in principle or practice; deviating from divine law; addicted to vice; sinful; immoral. Each of these definitions very clearly fit today's social media and also fits the founding and continuing practices of Facebook.

People should not be supporting these kinds of sites!

Your name on these sites is what brings them their money. You should not be sitting with these vain people; you should not be going with these dissemblers, you should not be a part of this congregation and you should not be sitting with the wicked!

Psalms 9:17 The wicked shall be turned into hell, and all the nations that forget God.

CHAPTER 18

OUR LIPS ARE NOT OUR OWN

Psalms 12:3-4 The LORD shall cut off all flattering lips, and the tongue that speaketh proud things: Who have said, With our tongue will we prevail; **our lips are our own**: who is lord over us?

Mankind has always had the problem of thinking too much of the ideas that they personally have over the words and commandments of God. Their opinion is what matters to them the most. Those that agree with them are the brilliant ones; those that disagree have mental problems. Why? They said it so it must be so! With their tongues they must prevail, the feel that their lips are their own. No one can tell them what to say or do.

God teaches us just the opposite. Our ideas and our words are not what are important. What is important is what God's Word says.

Romans 3:3-4 For what if some did not believe? shall their unbelief make the faith of God without effect? God forbid: yea, **let God be true,** but **every man a liar**; as it is written, That thou mightest be justified in thy sayings, and mightest overcome when thou art judged.

Psalms 100:5 For the LORD is good; his mercy is everlasting; and **his truth endureth to all generations.**

Psalms 119:160 Thy word is true from the beginning: and every one of thy righteous judgments **endureth for ever.**

We could argue back and forth with our opinions forever and never come to an agreement. What we need to realize is that the only time we are right is when we agree with God Almighty! One thing is certain; all of us have been and will be wrong. As humans we can be lying when we truly feel we are telling the truth. We make mistakes!

God does not make mistakes.

Hebrews 6:18 That by two immutable things, in which it was **impossible for God to lie**, we might have a strong consolation, who have fled for refuge to lay hold upon the hope set before us:

Titus 1:2 In hope of eternal life, which God, that cannot lie, promised before the world began;

From the time I was a teenager my life verse has been Proverbs 3:5-6 Trust in the LORD with all thine heart; and lean not unto thine own understanding. In all thy ways acknowledge him, and he shall direct thy paths. Thankfully, I learned early in life not to go by my own feelings, but by the Word of God. There are many things that I still don't understand but I believe that God does, so I want to do what He says not what I feel.

When He directs our path we know we will end up in the right place, but when we follow our own instincts, we will end up getting ourselves in trouble. We can never figure out everything so we must learn to rely on God and His Word.

In today's communication world, people are becoming hooked on their own ideas and words. When you are on the web, look at the news stories and then look at all of the comments that are being made. Look at all of the thumbs up and the thumbs down! Never before have had people the opportunity to express their opinion so much and to see what others think of their opinion.

Like the people mentioned in Psalms 12, they feel that their lips are their own. Who has the right to control their words? Like it or not, God does have the right to control us!

We were made by Him and for Him. We will give account to Him one day of every word we have ever used.

Matthew 12:36-37 But I say unto you, That every idle word that men shall speak, they shall give account thereof in the day of judgment. For by thy words thou shalt be justified, and by thy words thou shalt be condemned.

The Psalmist David recognized the problem in his day. Psalms 12:1-3 Help, LORD; for the godly man ceaseth; for the faithful fail from among the children of men. They speak vanity every one with his neighbour: with flattering lips and with a double heart do they speak. The LORD shall cut off all flattering lips, and the tongue that speaketh proud things:

He saw that the Godly and the faithful groups were growing smaller and smaller while the vain talkers were expanding greatly. This is now happening at a greater pace than David could have ever imagined. With our cell phones, our texting, our computers and our social media to help; people are now more in love with their opinions than ever before!

I recently saw a news program about people who are still texting even when they are asleep. Another story told of cities in Europe that are padding their telephone poles because people are so caught up in their communications on their phones that they are bumping into the poles. Some places have made it illegal to text and drive, now some are considering making it illegal to walk and text because people have been injured and even killed walking out into traffic.

Many are so caught up in this self flattering social communication that they fail to communicate with God. They have missed out on the best communication with their friends and family (and it is not on Facebook but it is face to face!) That is the best kind of communication.

CHAPTER 19

ACCEPTABLE COMMUNICATIONS

Psalms 19:14 Let the words of my mouth, and the meditation of my heart, be acceptable in thy sight, O LORD, my strength, and my redeemer.

The one each of us should desire to accept us as a friend, is our Lord. For this to happen we must learn to communicate within the realm that our God has set for us. Since God is interested in the words from our mouths and even the meditations of our hearts, I am sure that He is interested in our posts and our texts. Everything we do should be acceptable in the sight of our God.

1 Timothy 2:1-3 I exhort therefore, that, first of all, supplications, prayers, intercessions, and giving of thanks, be made for all men; For kings, and for all that are in authority; that we may **lead a quiet and peaceable life in all godliness and honesty**. For this is good and **acceptable in the sight of God our Saviour;**

Notice that He wants us to pray for people, intercede for people and give thanks for people. He wants our lives to be quiet, peaceable, godly and honest. These are the things that are acceptable to God.

I can't prove it but I believe that if all of the communications on these social web sites fit these categories just mentioned; they would more than likely go out of business very soon. Sadly people are more interested in the things that are acceptable in their own sight instead of God's.

Ephesians 5:3-11 But fornication, and all uncleanness, or covetousness, **let it not be once named among you**, as becometh saints; Neither filthiness, nor **foolish talking**, nor jesting, which are not convenient: but rather giving of thanks. For this ye know, that no whoremonger, nor unclean person, nor covetous man, who is an idolater, hath any inheritance in the kingdom of Christ and of God. Let no man deceive you with **vain words:** for because of these things cometh the wrath of God upon the children of disobedience. **Be not ye therefore partakers with them.** For ye were sometimes darkness, but now are ye light in the Lord: walk as children of light: (For the fruit of the Spirit is in all goodness and righteousness and truth;) **Proving what is acceptable unto the Lord.** And **have no fellowship with the unfruitful works of darkness**, but rather reprove them.

These verses spell it out very clearly. We are to carefully watch what we communicate about and who we communicate with. Not once are we supposed to be involved with these unclean things. Even if we ourselves do not say the bad things we are not to be partakers with them that do. We are to produce the fruit of the Spirit and prove what is acceptable unto our Lord. Have no fellowship with the unfruitful works of darkness.

The last phrase in the verse is what I have attempted to do in this book. That is to reprove them. The word *reprove* means; "to convince of a fault, or to make it manifest."

I believe with all my heart that in the years to come we will continue to see the terrible effects of these social medias. Even among those who attempt to do things in a safe manor. God gives us some wonderful direction when it comes to acceptable communications.

Philippians 4:8 Finally, brethren, whatsoever things are true, whatsoever things are honest, whatsoever things are just, whatsoever things are pure, whatsoever things are lovely, whatsoever things are of good report; if there be any virtue, and if there be any praise, think on these things.

We must understand that what we read, what we hear and what we talk about are the things that are in our minds. God is telling us that we should not only be careful about our actual communications but we should be so careful that we are constantly aware of how these things affect our thinking.

If you are sprayed by a skunk the smell will stick to you and when you are communicating with the evil of this world it is going to attach itself to you in some way.

We must be very aware of the dangers. We should do all we can to avoid these things.

I don't think anyone would want a skunk to spray them; neither should we want our lives to smell of the stench of this world and its dirty communication.

God has told us to think only on the things that are true, honest, just, pure, lovely, and of a good report. I'm sorry but you cannot be reading things on these sites that are just the opposite of this command without those evil things becoming a part of your thought life. I want you look at the definition of the word, "*think.*"

Think: To have the mind occupied on some subject; to have idea, or to resolve ideas in the mind; to judge; to conclude; to hold as a settled opinion; to imagine; to suppose; to fancy; to muse; to meditate, to reflect; to recollect, to call to mind; to presume; to believe; to esteem.

Now look at another verse that deals with our thought life and look at the definitions.

Psalms 143:5 I remember the days of old; I meditate on all thy works; I muse on the work of thy hands.

Remember: To have in mind an idea which had been in mind before, and which recurs to the mind without effort; when we use an effort to recall an idea; to preserve the memory of; to preserve from keeping from being forgotten.

Psalms 77:11 I will remember the works of the LORD: surely I will remember thy wonders of old.

Ecclesiastes 12:1 Remember now thy Creator in the days of thy youth, while the evil days come not, nor the years draw nigh, when thou shalt say, I have no pleasure in them;

Meditate: To dwell on any thing in thought; to contemplate; to study; to turn or revolve any subject in the mind.

Psalms 77:12 I will meditate also of all thy work, and talk of thy doings.

Psalms 1:1-2 Blessed is the man that walketh not in the counsel of the ungodly, nor standeth in the way of sinners, nor sitteth in the seat of the scornful. But his delight is in the law of the LORD; and in his law doth he meditate day and night.

Muse: Deep thought; close attention or contemplation which abstracts the mind from passing scenes; hence sometimes absence of mind; to ponder; to think closely; to study in silence.

Isaiah 26:3 Thou wilt keep him in perfect peace, whose mind is stayed on thee: because he trusteth in thee.

God is telling us that our thought life should be focused on Him and His Word, not on the worthless garbage of this world. People today are so busy posting and texting that they have lost the art of thinking, remembering, meditating and musing. Who needs to think when all the things of this world are available to you with the touch of a few buttons?

Proverbs 23:7 For as he thinketh in his heart, so is he: Eat and drink, saith he to thee; but his heart is not with thee.

We are what we think about! This should cause everyone to stop and consider what their minds are occupied with. We must remember that it is not just what we say and do that we will be judged for but also for what goes on in our minds.

It seems in this age of fast communication that people have lost what was once considered ethical communications. People are posting things that they have heard or seen much too quickly.

I recently heard about a situation where there was a tragedy in a family and before the family could contact others and break the news to them in a gentle manner, a person that was not a part of the family posted the story on Facebook and several family members were shocked and hurt by the news and also hurt by the fact that many others learned of the problem before they did.

To me this is not acceptable communications. Some things are private and just because you see or hear something and you have a phone that you can get the news out on quickly do not give you that right. There was an old saying that I believe still should be used today, "It's none of your business!"

I have also heard many complaints about people posting photos of other people without their permission. It is sad to me that images that were meant only for friends and family are now being viewed by the world. I remember hearing about living in glass houses but now it seems we are living in a glass world. Almost nothing is considered private anymore.

In this book I have quoted over two hundred and sixty verses that deal with communication and there are many more in the Bible. If our God thought so much about this subject I believe it is very important for each of us to pay very close attention to it.

We must realize how fast things are changing and how good Satan is at using these things for his own purpose.

Proverbs 10:32 The lips of the righteous know what is acceptable: but the mouth of the wicked speaketh frowardness.

It is our job to determine through the scripture what acceptable communication is. Whether you agree with what has been written or not, understand that each of us will one day stand before our all knowing, all powerful, and ever present God. We will give an account to Him based on what He says not based on how we feel.

Ecclesiastes 12:10 The preacher sought to find out acceptable words: and that which was written was upright, even words of truth.

This has been my attempt to find acceptable words, words that guide you into truth and away from evil. As a pastor, I have had to deal with many difficult situations in my ministry. Problems have always been around, but sadly social media has multiplied them tremendously. The things I have already dealt with have made my heart to ache, but even more the things I see coming make my heart ache. Knowing that many who have heard me teach these things, cannot pull themselves away from them. They have become so addicted they cannot stop what they are doing, even when they see the bad results!

God help us all to do our best to do what is acceptable in His sight! Help us to understand just what it is that God expects from His people.

Deuteronomy 10:12-13 And now, Israel, what doth the LORD thy God require of thee, but to fear the LORD thy God, to walk in all his ways, and to love him, and to serve the LORD thy God with all thy heart and with all thy soul, To keep the commandments of the LORD, and his statutes, which I command thee this day **for thy good?**

It would be wonderful if God's people could become as attached to Him and to communication with Him as they are attached to their phones and computers. God requires us to fear Him, to walk in His ways, to love Him, to serve Him with all of our heart and soul and to keep His commandments. This should not be looked at as a burden but as a wonderful privilege. Notice that God tells us that doing these things are for "our good." If there is anyone that we should want as a friend, it should be our God.

James 2:23 And the scripture was fulfilled which saith, Abraham believed God, and it was imputed unto him for righteousness: and **he was called the Friend of God.**

Abraham was a man who had such a relationship with God that the Lord looked on him as a friend. What an honor! We know God is our friend, but to have God consider us His friend is one of the greatest complements that we could ever receive.

I pray that everyone who reads this book would accept God's request for our friendship. Not just a click on a web site button but a real change in our hearts and in our lives.

2 Corinthians 5:17 Therefore if any man be in Christ, he is a new creature: old things are passed away; behold, all things are become new.

CHAPTER 20

FIXING THE PROBLEM

One of the most difficult things that have to happen for a problem to be fixed is to admit that you have a problem. Many in this world never come to Christ for salvation because they never see themselves as a lost sinner headed for an eternity in hell.

Romans 3:23 For all have sinned, and come short of the glory of God;

Revelation 20:15 And whosoever was not found written in the book of life was cast into the lake of fire.

Sadly, people see themselves only from this worldly perspective and not from the eyes of Almighty God.

Matthew 7:22-23 Many will say to me in that day, Lord, Lord, have we not prophesied in thy name? and in thy name have cast out devils? and in thy name done many wonderful works? And then will I profess unto them, I never knew you: depart from me, ye that work iniquity.

These people saw themselves as prophets and workers for the Lord but they had never had the most important realization. They are sinners who need a Saviour. They also need to understand that the only Saviour is the Lord Jesus Christ.

John 14:6 Jesus saith unto him, I am the way, the truth, and the life: no man cometh unto the Father, but by me.

Acts 4:12 Neither is there salvation in any other: for there is none other name under heaven given among men, whereby we must be saved.

Ask yourself this question. "If I were to die right now, do I know for sure that I will go to Heaven?" Most people think so, or hope so but God wants us to know for sure.

1 John 5:11-13 And this is the record, that God hath given to us eternal life, and this life is in his Son. He that hath the Son hath life; and he that hath not the Son of God hath not life. These things have I written unto you that believe on the name of the Son of God; **that ye may know that ye have eternal life,** and that ye may believe on the name of the Son of God.

Our faith in God must be based on the Word of God. Many religions today base their faith on their traditions or on their personal experiences. God wants us to base our beliefs and our faith on His Word.

John 5:39 Search the scriptures; for in them ye think ye have eternal life: and they are they which testify of me.

For true salvation to come to a life, the person must make a confession of their sin and a commitment of their heart to the Lord.

Romans 10:9-10 That if thou shalt confess with thy mouth the Lord Jesus, and shalt believe in thine heart that God hath raised him from the dead, thou shalt be saved. For with the heart man believeth unto righteousness; and with the mouth confession is made unto salvation.

Many religious people will miss Heaven by just a foot. They know about God in their head but they have never accepted Him into their heart.

This is the same problem many will have with their attachments and addictions to these social networks. They cannot see that they have a problem, so the problem will not get fixed.

Just like the sinner that cannot see that they are headed for hell, many people that are on these sites cannot see themselves and their families headed for the disaster that may be just around the corner.

Quoted in this book were hundreds of scriptures that God gave us to awaken us to the dangers of this kind of communication. Nearly every week we hear on the news of terrible disasters taking place in people's lives because of the internet. Yet, people still can't see the problem.

2 Corinthians 4:4 In whom the god of this world hath blinded the minds of them which believe not, lest the light of the glorious gospel of Christ, who is the image of God, should shine unto them.

Just as Satan wants to keep people from salvation, he also wants to keep people from fixing these other problems. If people are focused on themselves and their own pleasures, he knows that they will never accomplish the things that God wants to do with their lives.

My hope and prayer is that everyone will see that Facebook and other social media is a problem. That God's people should stop wasting their time, talent, and treasure on things that are empty and worthless. Just because something is very popular with the world, does not make it a good thing. In fact, the opposite is true. God warns us that the way of the world leads to destruction and that the right way to go is traveled by the few.

Matthew 7:13-14 Enter ye in at the strait gate: for wide is the gate, and broad is the way, that leadeth to destruction, and many there be which go in thereat: Because strait is the gate, and narrow is the way, which leadeth unto life, and few there be that find it.

Can you see your problem? Do you know which way you are going? Please pray and ask the Lord to guide you in the right direction.

1 Corinthians 2:10-13 But God hath revealed them unto us by his Spirit: for the Spirit searcheth all things, yea, the deep things of God. For what man knoweth the things of a man, save the spirit of man which is in him? even so the things of God knoweth no man, but the Spirit of God. Now we have received, not the spirit of the world, but the spirit which is of God; that we might know the things that are freely given to us of God. Which things also we speak, not in the words which man's wisdom teacheth, but which the Holy Ghost teacheth; comparing spiritual things with spiritual.

John 16:13 Howbeit when he, the Spirit of truth, is come, he will guide you into all truth: for he shall not speak of himself; but whatsoever he shall hear, that shall he speak: and he will shew you things to come.

www.ingramcontent.com/pod-product-compliance
Lightning Source LLC
LaVergne TN
LVHW092007050326
832904LV00017B/314/J